Ocean Is a Nine Year Old Dirt Bike Girl

By Ocean

FOR MY 'OHANA

ISBN 978-0-578-79898-1

Library of Congress Control Number:
2020922002

First Edition: 2020

Martina Dodson
PO Box 11762
Lahaina, HI
96761
For more information:
info@martinadodson.com
Instagram: #Ocean.247

Printed in the U.S.A.

ALOHA!

Aloha is how we say hello in Hawaii. Aloha has many meanings. For instance, it can also mean goodbye. For me, Aloha means living the life you love.

This is a true story about me, Ocean. I am a super duper happy nine year old dirt bike girl who lives on the island of Maui in Hawaii. Every day here is like an adventure. This story is about how I first started dirt bike racing, and about my grom life on Maui. I want all kids to know that you're never too young to dream

BIG!

My life as *Ocean* started in my mom's belly. She would go surfing and snowboarding when I was just the size of an orange. Maybe that's where my love for going fast first started.

You might be wondering why my name is Ocean. When I was born, both my parents instinctively knew I would be wild and free just like the Ocean which happens to be where they met while surfing.

I also have a little sister named *Coral.* She is five, and she is the boss in the family or at least that's what she thinks. Coral was named after the coral reef, which gives life to the ocean. I always make sure to take care of my sister because she is amazing. I have also learned to take care of the coral reef by doing things like wearing reef-friendly sunscreen. I do this because the coral reef is amazing, too!

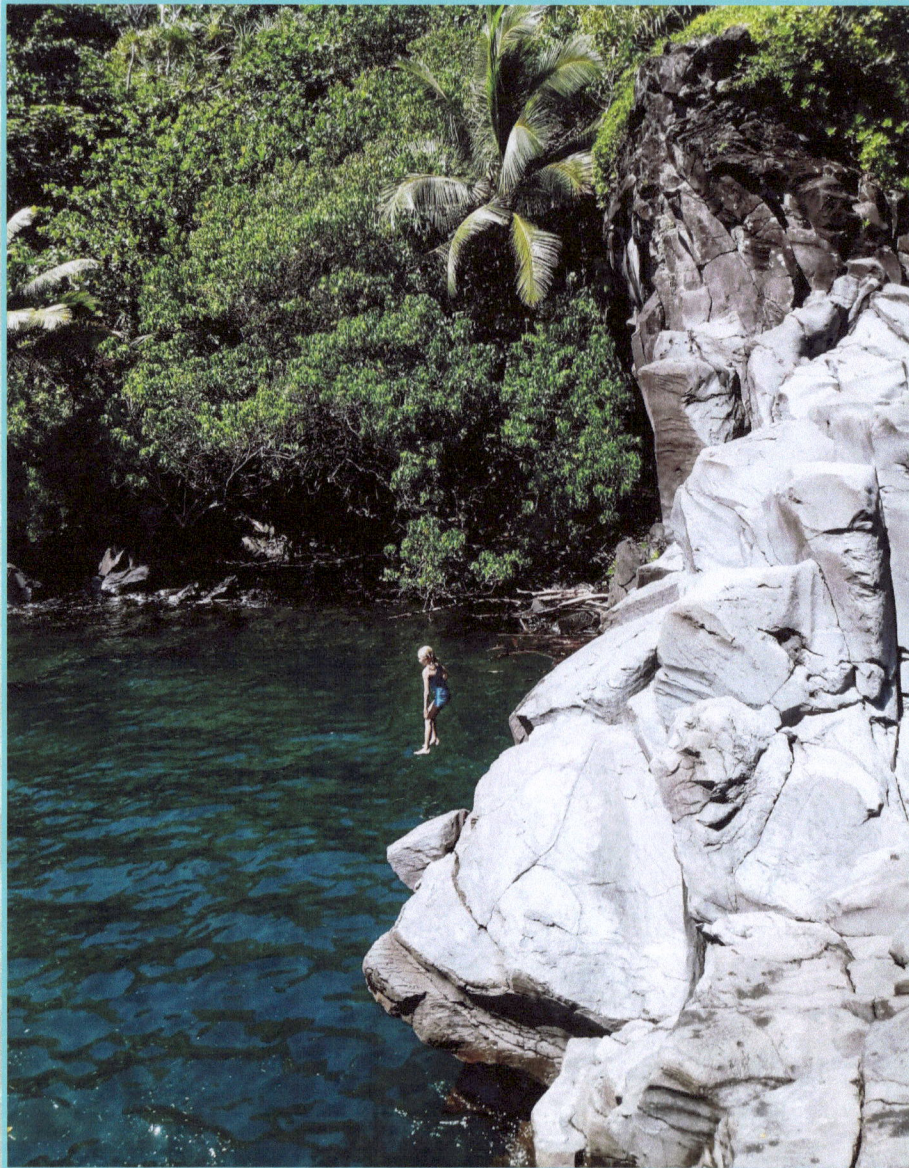

Being nine years old and growing up in Hawaii is really, really cool, fun, and always exciting. There are so many great things to do out in nature. My favorite activities are playing mermaid, surfing, jumping off waterfalls, fishing, horseback riding, snorkeling, ripsticking, hiking, whale watching, swimming with dolphins and turtles, and of course, my absolute number one favorite activity/sport is...wait for

it... *dirtbiking!*

It is just so, so, so much *fun going fast*, racing, and jumping

really, really high up in the air! There are many awesome dirt trails in Maui, including tough off-road trails, and are also lots of places to explore in the mountains and jungle. We also have a really cool track here where we race!

Hula dancing is something we practice inside for a change. I have been dancing for a few years now, and I love it. When we perform at various events, we get to dress up in real hula outfits and make our own plumeria leis. We also make our own ti leaf skirts. Phew! Our hula outfits are hard to make, and are very time consuming. Doing this requires a lot of leaf and flower picking, and then you have to tie them all together with string. But the leis and skirts look beautiful once you are done, and they are what the Hawaiians have worn for many years for traditional dancing.

Okay, now back to the story of how I became a dirt bike girl…

When I was just a baby, my dad would put me in front of him on his dirt bike and ride up in the mountains. The mountains are spectacular, and the view from their height is breathtaking.

At age three, I got my first real dirt bike with training wheels. Being a determined, fearless kid, I would drive it super fast in the

neighborhood while shouting *"Braaap!"*

At age four, I received my first trophy. It was a big thrill! I also got rewarded by getting ice cream after the race was over.

My first dirt bike was a PW50, and the next size one was a KTM 50. My new dirt bike is called a KTM 65. I can barely reach the ground with my feet, but that's fine with me because it goes really, really fast!

I love racing!

My racing number is 247. I picked that number because I always want to dirt bike 24 hours a day, 7 days a week. Racing is exciting, and sometimes I get a bit nervous especially when I race in front of big crowds, where many kids want to win first place. But for me, racing is so much more than just winning. Racing is exhilarating because it allows me to travel, see amazing places, make new friends, and ride all the time! We don't have any amusement parks in Hawaii, but I think racing is like riding a really, really cool roller coaster!

I love it.

My biggest race was last year at the *KTM junior supercross challenge* in Atlanta, Georgia. I traveled there with my dad. I got to race in front of 70,000 people at the Mercedes-Benz stadium.

After the big race, I got to sign autographs, and Motocross companies gave me sponsored items like shirts, stickers, and hats.

It was so much fun!

To be really good at dirt biking, *I have to train almost every day.* This is physically demanding and requires a great deal of concentration and technical skill.

My dad, my dirt bike friends, and I usually train by riding at the dirt bike track.

It is also fun to ride up in the mountains, but the trails can get very steep. When riding on off-road trails, it is always good to have a

riding buddy in case anything happens to the rider or the dirt bike.

My dad is the best riding buddy ever because I know I can always trust him to be watching out for me, and he is really good at fixing dirt bikes.

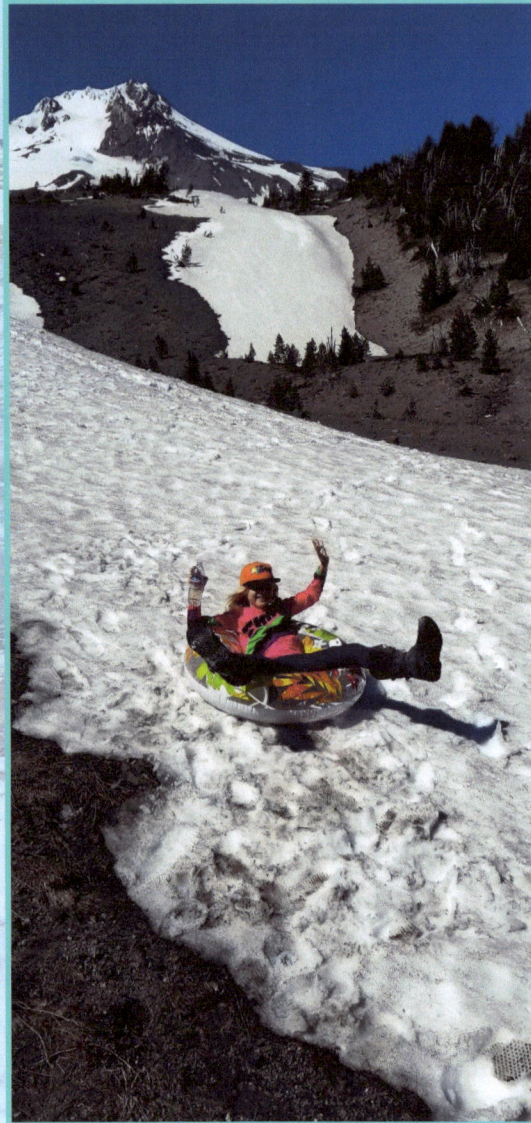

Another fun fact about me is that I also have a really big 'Ohana.

'Ohana means family in Hawaiian.

On Maui, everyone is pretty much family. I have a pet cat I call my brother. His name is Baker, and he is so cute. He is named after Mount Baker in Washington and was born the same year as me. Dad, mom, Coral and I travel to Mount Baker in Washington, and to Mount Hood in Oregon for vacations as a family.

I also have a grandma cat, she is 85 years old in cat years. Her birthday is on Halloween and her name is Liten.

Liten means small in Swedish.

My mom is from Sweden, and she tries to teach me Swedish, but it's a pretty hard language to learn. I do know how to say ice cream in Swedish, though!

There are kids in Sweden who also enjoy dirt biking like me, and they have races there, too. Also the Swedish Pippi Longstocking stories are my favorite stories. In one of the chapters from Pippi's book where it was Pippi's birthday she would stick her whole face in the middle of the cake, eating it that way. Ever since I heard that story, I've been eating my birthday cake the same way. It is so fun, but a bit messy.

I also had a pet *gecko* that I called my cousin, but he ran away.

Hawaii has many geckos, and they make loud sounds. If you hold your hand up in a fist, make a little hole in between your thumb and pointy finger, and make a kissing sound, it will sound just like a gecko.

Since my pet gecko ran away, we added two new members to our
'Ohana.

Our two new members are a couple of baby goats. I am so stoked about our new baby goats. Our baby goats' names are Lily and Coffee and they are adorable.

I love the ocean!

Besides riding dirt bikes, Coral and I love playing mermaids. We jump in the ocean and put our mermaid fins on. The fin looks just like real mermaid fins. *I can swim really fast with my fin* and dive deep down where the sea life is amazing.

There are really spectacular tropical fish underwater, and sometimes a Hawaiian green sea turtle will pop up right next to us to say *Aloha.* They are so adorable and big, but also very graceful. When they swim, it's like they are flying underwater. It is magical under the surface of the ocean. Coral and I find all kinds of treasures there, like unique shells and beautiful coral pieces.

When we are free diving in the ocean, we can hear the whales singing their songs to each other. Sometimes a dolphin will squeak a bit, too. It's super fun to make yourself sound like a dolphin underwater, too. You should try it one day if you haven't yet. I will tell you all about more of our adventures next time.

But for now, I have to go. It's time to train on my dirt bike. Remember to always dream BIG! Braaap!

Aloha,

Ocean

Lily and Coffee.

We love hanging out at the beach!

A grom is a young participant in extreme sports.

Hibiscus.

Always dream BIG!

ALOHA!

www.ingramcontent.com/pod-product-compliance
Lightning Source LLC
Chambersburg PA
CBHW041245040426
42445CB00005B/147